This is My Chair

Written by Helen Dineen

Illustrated by Charlie Alder

Collins

This is my chair. It's soft and snug.

2

No! Scram! This splendid chair is just for me.

Stop right there! That's not a chair.
Jump down.

4

That's a good spot. You must sit in that chair.

Stop! I will not let you mess up my plans.

It's not hard to understand.
Just sit tight. Got it?

Pack it in! Stop pestering me and just keep still.

Now it's too dark. I cannot see my book. Help!

Wow! A night light. What a perfect gift. Thank you.

This will do the trick. Click!
That's much better.

Wait! This blanket is for you.
Join me. I insist.

Now curl up next to me. All's well that ends well!

This is my chair

:paw: Review: After reading :paw:

Use your assessment from hearing the children read to choose any GPCs, words or tricky words that need additional practice.

Read 1: Decoding

- Talk about the meaning of **right** and **tight** in context.
  - o Point to **right** on page 4, and ask the children to think about the meaning of the word as they read the page. Ask: What does "**right** there!" mean? (*exactly there, on that exact spot*)
  - o Point to **tight** on page 7. Ask: What does "sit **tight**" mean here? (*sit very still*)
- Encourage the children to read these words by sounding out each letter and blending. Check they sound out adjacent consonants clearly, such as "t" and "r" in **trick**.

  trick   blanket   insist   click   splendid   plans

- Point to the words **soft** then **snug** on page 2. Say: Can you blend in your head when you read these words? Then ask the children to read all of page 3, using the same method.

Read 2: Prosody

- On pages 4 and 5, encourage the children to emphasise words to clarify where or what the bear is talking about.
- Model reading page 4, emphasising the words **there** and **That's**, and pointing. Repeat for **that** on page 5.
- Encourage the children to read the pages, emphasising the words, and pointing as if they were the bear.

Read 3: Comprehension

- Ask the children if they like special "soft and snug" places to sit and read. Where do they most like to sit and relax? Why?
- Talk about the title and front cover picture.
  - o Ask: Whose chair is it at the beginning of the story?
  - o Ask: Whose is it at the end? Talk about the picture on page 13, and the idea that they are sharing.
- Turn to pages 14 and 15, and use the objects in the picture as prompts for the children to retell the story.
  - o Ask: Who was sitting on this big chair at first? (*the bear*) Where did the bear want the rabbit to sit? (*the small chair*)
  - o Point to the night light, and ask: Who gave the night light to the bear, and why? (*the rabbit, because it was too dark to read*)
  - o Point to the blanket and ask: Where was the blanket in the end? (*over the bear and rabbit*)